D1578568

OCEAN EXPLORER

Written by Fiona Waters

Illustrated by Celia Witchard

HENDERSON
PUBLISHING LTD

WATER, WATER EVERYWHERE

Whenever you dip a toe into the sea, you are connecting with ALL the world's oceans, because the earth's sea water is one continuous mass. Over two-thirds of the entire earth's surface is covered by sea water! Pretty awesome, huh?

THAT'S SOME STORM!
Today's oceans began to fill up in the last 200 million years of the earth's history. As the early earth cooled, *water vapour* condensed and formed storm clouds, from which rain fell and eventually made oceans.

WHAT'S WHERE
The five oceans in the world are the Pacific, the Atlantic, the Indian, the Southern and the Arctic. The Arctic is the smallest and its centre is permanently covered by a layer of sea ice. Brrrr!

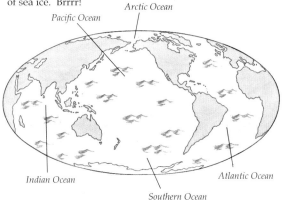

Arctic Ocean

Pacific Ocean

Indian Ocean

Southern Ocean

Atlantic Ocean

The largest ocean is the Pacific Ocean. It covers 165,384,000 sq km (63,855,000 sq miles) – more than one third of the earth!

WATERY MIND-BOGGLERS

Here are some more mind-boggling ocean figures to get your head round!

- Total surface area – 362,000,000 sq km (139,800,000 sq miles)

- Average depth – 3.5 km (2.2 miles)

- Temperature range – 1.9°C to 36°C (28°F to 97°F)

- Deepest known point – 10,920 m (35,827 ft)

- Highest recorded wave – 34 m (112 ft) from trough to crest, recorded in 1933

FACT OR FICTION?

Many early sailors were terrified of creatures that they believed lived in the oceans. There are many weird and wonderful stories of strange and sinister monsters coming up out of the deep.

LET'S EXPLORE

People have always been fascinated by the sea, both above and below the surface, but it is only fairly recently that we have been able to explore the sea properly. Way back in time, water travel took a while to catch on.

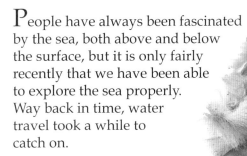

STAYING AT HOME

Thousands of years ago, people did not travel very far away from their homes. They could make all their own tools, and they could weave and spin cloth or use animal skins for clothes. They also grew crops and kept animals for food.

Small flint axe

Animal skin

MOVING ON

Gradually, people realised that they could trade goods and skills with other people, and they began to go further afield.

WATER TRANSPORT

Early traders were not put off by little things like rivers. They simply invented water transport!

Indonesian log boat

Small mallet for driving in wooden pegs

Tool for fine hollowing

Early water travel was as easy as falling off a log...but people became fed up with wet clothes, so they hollowed out the log and sat inside instead! The first explorers were launched.

BELIEVE IT OR NOT...

Before the discovery that the world was round, sailors used to fear that they would fall off the edge if they sailed beyond the horizon. Whoops!

A LIFE ON THE OCEAN WAVE

Travelling by water was so convenient that it soon became commonplace.

EGYPTIAN SAILORS

According to Egyptian priests, the world was a flat rectangle, and the heavens were held up by massive pillars at each corner. However, when Queen Hatshepsut sent ships as far away as the Indian Ocean...not a pillar in sight! The priests said that the pillars must be further away than they thought. Sneaky!

The Egyptians' first boats were made of the stalks of papyrus plants bunched together, but later they used cedar wood.

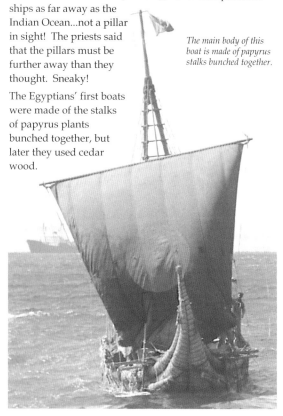

The main body of this boat is made of papyrus stalks bunched together.

Roman Adventurers

The Romans kept their oarsmen up to scratch. A musician played the flute to keep them in time as they rowed.

Without compasses or maps, Roman sailors needed to keep the shore in sight all the time, but the wind could blow them on to the rocks. Sailing was a dangerous business in ancient times!

Animal Trade

Roman merchant navy ships were capable of travelling vast distances with huge cargoes on board. Transporting everything from fish sauce to wild animals, working on board could be an eye-opening business.

Roman merchant ship

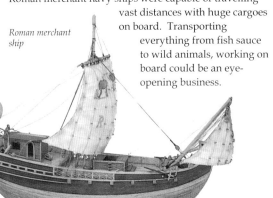

Wild animals were collected from many countries and taken to the Colosseum in Rome. Fancy sharing a cabin with a tiger or a rhinoceros! Putting on a good show was so important to the emperors that they spent vast sums of money on this horrible trade.

Bold Voyagers

Whether fierce fighters or just plain curious, many bold voyagers took to the seas to discover and claim more of the world for themselves.

Vikings v the World

For 300 years, from the 8th to 11th centuries, the Vikings took on the world. They were brilliant sailors and their wooden *longships* used to strike terror into hearts wherever they were seen.

Fierce Beasts

The Vikings often carved fierce beasts on the *prow* of their ships to scare their enemies as they landed, and their sails were dyed blood red. Oo-er!

Dressed to Kill

Many of the romantic images of Vikings are wrong. For example, they didn't wear horned helmets, but round caps of iron or leather!

Warriors prepared for battle by putting on bearskin cloaks and working themselves up into a fearful frenzy.

Dead Wealthy

The richest Vikings were buried in ships together with their clothes, weapons and furniture. Unfortunately, their servants and even their dogs were killed and also put into the ship, which was then set alight.

TO BOLDLY GO...

Henry the Navigator (1394-1460), the first of the great ocean voyagers, only sailed a few times himself! He seemed to prefer dry land, but he did finance many of the earliest voyages of exploration.

The first European to sail to India was Vasco da Gama, who was shown the way by an Arab pilot who taught him to use the monsoon winds. Handy, eh!

THE MAP MAN

Christopher Columbus (1451-1506) discovered America in 1492, only he thought that it was China! How wrong can you get?

Christopher Columbus' ship – Santa Maria

In 1508, the Italian navigator Amerigo Vespucci was made Chief Royal Pilot of Spain and things improved on the navigating front. All Spanish sea captains had to report back to him so that he could bring his maps up to date.

Before proper maps, sailors had to navigate by the stars. Difficult in the daytime!

PIRATES

In times past, if pirates appeared over the horizon, the best policy would have been to scarper! Here's why...

JOLLY ROGER

The feared pirate flag, the Jolly Roger, had many variations. It indicated that the pirates would show no mercy, and walking the plank would be the end for many a victim.

A BETTER LIFE

Many pirate crews were made up of formerly honest seamen who were fed up with eating maggoty biscuits, sharing their bunks with rats and being lashed with the *cat-o'-nine-tails*. Well, wouldn't you be?

BELIEVE IT OR NOT...

One of the most terrifying pirates, Blackbeard, even used to scare his own crew! He stuck burning cords into his hat when he went into battle, and carried six pistols. Fierce, or what!

FEMALE FIENDS
Not all pirates were men! Several brave women disguised themselves as men and threw themselves into a life of fighting and adventure.

BURIED TREASURE – DREAMS OR TRUTH?
Pirates used to divide their booty more or less equally, although fights always broke out. One crewman was given a single large diamond instead of several smaller ones. Not happy with this, he smashed his big one into small pieces with a hammer!

Gold doubloon

'Piece of eight' or Spanish peso

Best of all was Spanish gold or silver – a gold *doubloon* was worth about seven weeks' pay. Rich pickings indeed!

X MARKS THE SPOT
Brimming treasure chests buried according to parchment maps are mostly romantic myths, but William Kidd (1645-1701) did bury some of his ill-gotten gains near what is now New York. His map must have been good because someone else dug up all the treasure!

Discovering Shipwrecks

Many thousands of ships lie at the bottom of the ocean – most lost for ever, with their positions unknown. Curious divers have attempted to discover and explore the sunken remains.

Famous Disaster

When the Titanic set sail on her maiden voyage, she was considered unsinkable. But on the night of 14 April 1912, she hit an iceberg and sank with the loss of 1,503 lives.

Plane Remains

It isn't just ships that sit on the bottom – aeroplanes can crash into the sea too. There is an area in the Atlantic Ocean called the Bermuda Triangle where many planes and ships have mysteriously disappeared.

Distinctly Daft Diving Devices

Some of the earliest diving equipment seems to have come from the world of fantasy, such as this primitive diving suit. Other inventions were more sensible, like the early diving bell. Four people could sit on the sea-bed in it for 90 minutes.

Dangerous, primitive diving suit

SERIOUSLY HEAVY!

The most important parts of
early diving suits were the
very heavy metal helmet
and the lead-soled boots.
You couldn't run far
wearing that lot!

*Lead-soled diving boots
and diving helmet from
around 1840*

FREE-FLOATING

A Frenchman, Jacques Cousteau, invented the aqualung in
1943. This was a huge advance – for the first time ever, a
diver could go as deep as 30 m (98 ft) without being
attached to a ship.

Dive, Dive, Dive!

The first submarines made underwater travel possible. They also became important as wartime fighting machines.

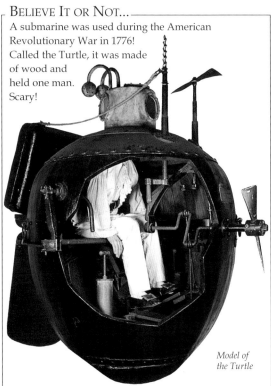

Model of the Turtle

Bottom Crawler

An underwater vehicle which could drive on the sea-bed was invented in 1894. It could go to depths of 6 m (20 ft), and the diver could get out and wander around.

LONG-DISTANCE TRAVEL

Modern submarines can run on nuclear power and are able to travel great distances before needing to refuel or surface. They have very sophisticated sonar systems to locate other vessels.

HMS Dreadnought was Britain's first nuclear-powered submarine and carried an 88-person crew underwater for weeks at a time. Its design was based on the shape of a whale!

HMS Dreadnought

BIG AND FAST

The Russians have the biggest and the fastest submarines in the world. The Typhoon type measures 170 m (558 ft) and the Alpha can probably exceed 42 knots when submerged.

No, a *knot* isn't just something you tie in a piece of string! It's the unit of speed used by ships and aircraft. One knot equals one nautical mile per hour.

Today's nuclear-powered submarines can carry high-powered torpedoes to fire at enemy vessels and are the most powerful weapon carriers ever.

SUBMERGED

People have been rocketed into space to explore what's out there, but the ocean depths are just as mysterious, with hidden places that remain undiscovered.

SUBMERSIBLES

Submersibles are like miniature submarines and are used for underwater exploration. They cannot travel far and have to be raised and lowered by a vessel on the water's surface.

The French submersible, Nautile

On deep dives, a submersible becomes very cold inside. The pressure outside is so enormous that the curved portholes, made of special glass, actually flatten!

SNORKELLING

If you don't fancy going quite so deep, how about snorkelling? It's dead simple. The snorkel, which is a tube with a mouthpiece attached, sticks out above the water. You just breathe normally, flap your flippers and off you go!

WHO GOES THERE?

Apart from all those snorkellers, submersibles and submarines, what else is wandering around the oceans? It all depends on how deep you go! The ocean is divided into zones, starting from the surface:

Sunlit zone: 0-200 m (0-660 ft) – lots of animals and plants

Twilight zone: 200-1,000 m (660-3,300 ft) – no more plants, but diving whales and octopuses!

Dark zone: 1,000-4,000 m (3,300-13,120 ft) – the weirdoes – angler fish and gulper eels...yuck!

Abyss: 4,000-6,000 m (13,120-19,700 ft) – very, very cold and very, very dark! Hot water bottles needed!

Trenches: Over 6,000 m (19,700 ft) – sea cucumbers... and no, these creatures won't make nice sandwiches!

TRENCHES

A *trench* is a deep valley on the ocean floor. The Mariana Trench, the deepest ever at 10,920 m (35,828 ft), could hold 28 Empire State Buildings standing on top of each other. That's some elevator ride!

BELIEVE IT OR NOT...

It would take 25 years for a dead shrimp to sink to the bottom of a deep trench. It CERTAINLY wouldn't be nice to eat by then!

GOING DOWN

There are some pretty weird creatures living in the dark depths of the world's oceans. They have developed in ways which help them to hunt and survive in the blackness.

Deep-sea hatchet

THE TWILIGHT ZONE

Things are pretty strange down here! Many fish have rows of lights on their undersides, to camouflage them against spots of light showing through from the world above. Seriously weird!

A deep-sea hatchet (not the kind you find in a tool box!), has huge eyes to help it spot its prey in the darkness.

The angler fish has a light at the end of a fin on its head which attracts an instant meal. Next time you go fishing, try this technique!

THE DARKEST DEPTHS

You would expect the fish here to keep bumping into each other! They are mostly black and the water is black too...and very, very cold. Brrrr...

Deep-sea fish, such as the angler fish, have huge mouths and stretchy stomachs, and have been found with fish twice their own size inside them, swallowed whole. Greedy guts!

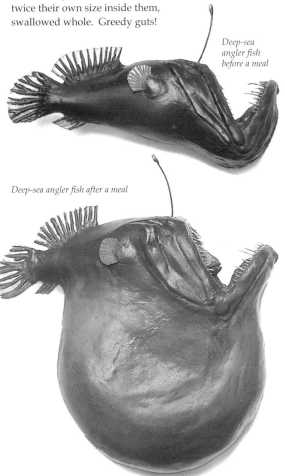

Deep-sea angler fish before a meal

Deep-sea angler fish after a meal

NOWHERE ELSE TO GO!

The bottom of the ocean is not a nice place to be. It is very dark and cold, and covered in ooze – yuck! The few animals around have extra long legs, like the sea spider whose legs are 80 cm (2 ft) across. NOT one to find in the bath!

Deep-sea cucumber

...And there are cucumbers on legs! Totally weird.

DEEP-SEA EARTHQUAKES

Earthquakes on the sea-bed cause tidal waves above called *tsunamis*. Once they hit the coast they cause terrible devastation.

The highest tsunami ever recorded was about 85 m (279 ft) tall and the fastest was travelling at 900 kph (559 mph). Phew!

ON THE MOVE

The ocean bed is constantly changing as the giant *plates* which make up the earth's surface shift about. *Lava* (hot, liquid rock) spouts up from the *crust* (the earth's outer layer) to form new ocean floor, and plates slide under each other.

SMOKERS

Smokers are like huge chimneys on the ocean floor. They spew out clouds of fantastically hot water – up to 400°C (752°F).

Smokers are home to a number of creatures. Tube worms up to 3 m (10 ft) long lurk around, together with giant clams. Whenever a vent stops producing water, the local wildlife has to set up home somewhere else.

Smoker

Tube worm

Home Sweet Home

The sea-bed is home to many plants and creatures. Here are a few of them...

Moving Home

The hermit crab steals other shells to live in. As it grows bigger, it has to find a larger shell to move into. It pulls its body out of the old shell and slips quickly into its new home.

This hermit crab is out of its shell – a vulnerable moment.

Weedy!

The sargassum fish lurks in clumps of sargassum seaweed. Frilly bits on its head and body make a crafty disguise, so predators can't spot it. Nifty, fishy!

D.I.Y.

Carrier shells are sea snails which stick bits of pebble, broken shells and even glass on to their own shells. It's not just decoration – it makes it jolly difficult for predators to get inside with that lot in the way!

STUCK FAST

Seaweeds are not weeds at all, but nutritious plants. They don't usually have roots – they hold on to rocks with root-like anchors called *holdfasts*. They can have a real tug of war with the waves!

SEAWEED AND CHIPS

Some people eat seaweed cooked like a vegetable. Eat up your greens? Double yuck!

Sugar kelp

Bladderwrack

Carragheen

Dulse

BELIEVE IT OR NOT...

In California there is a giant seaweed called kelp that can grow 1 m (3 ft) in a day, and reaches over 100 m (328 ft) in length.

HERE IS THE WEATHER FORECAST...

If you live near the sea, you can hang a piece of seaweed outside the back door and you will always know when you need an umbrella! If it is sunny, the seaweed will dry up, but when rain is coming, it will swell up again and feel damp.

She Sells Sea Shells

Whatever the shape or size of a shell that you find on the beach, it has been made by an animal, and it has grown outwards from the middle. The coil shapes made in this way can help you work out the age of the shell, a bit like the rings on a tree.

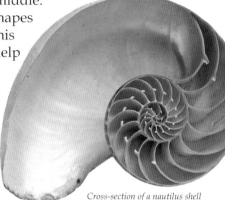

Cross-section of a nautilus shell

Snap!

The biggest shells of all are giant clams and they can weigh over 250 kg ($^1/_4$ tonne). They can be used as baths, but make sure you don't fall asleep! Living clams have killed divers by trapping their arms or legs.

Alive, Alive-O

Birds and sea otters eat the contents of shells...and so do humans! Scallops, mussels, clams and oysters are all delicious – and very good for you, as they are very low in calories but rich in protein. Yum, yum!

Oysters

Venus clams

Scallops

Mussels

True Grit

Next time you look at your granny's pearls, remember that a pearl comes from a very irritated creature! Whenever a tiny piece of grit becomes stuck in its shell, the animal will try to soothe the irritation by covering it with layers of *nacre*, a shelly material, and a pearl is born. Aah!

Black-lipped oyster

Not What They Seem

Tusk shells are nothing to do with elephants! They are shells which live with their heads always buried in the sand.

The slit-worm shell looks as if it has become unravelled! It can't move much, so it usually fixes itself to a rock.

Collecting Shells

If you have a collection of shells, make sure you store them in a box or drawer as they fade if they stay in the light for too long. Make sure you wash them out first, otherwise the pong will be too much!

Slit-worm shell

Hard Cases

Many sea creatures have hard cases and outer skeletons to protect their soft innards. Crabs and lobsters are hard-cased creatures, and so are beautiful coral reefs. Eh? Find out more...

Dry Bones
In warm, clear tropical waters, coral reefs cover huge areas. Coral is actually made up of masses of tiny anemone-like sea creatures, which make their own hard, outer skeleton to protect themselves.

The Biggest Coral Reef
Australia's Great Barrier Reef is the biggest coral reef in the world at over 2,000 km (1,250 miles) long. Millions of things live there, from fish to giant clams.

How Does Your Garden Grow?
The reefs look like gardens with plants and fronds everywhere. Some things that look like plants are actually animals! The lettuce slug breathes through its skin, which looks like a leaf. Salad, anyone?

Lettuce slug

ARMOUR-PLATING

Crabs and lobsters belong to a group of creatures called *crustaceans*. They have jointed shells, rather like the armour worn by medieval knights, to help them move.

BELIEVE IT OR NOT...

Because of the way a lobster's segments are joined together, it can only swim forwards or backwards. It cannot twist from side to side.

ANCIENT CREATURES

Trilobites were ancient sea creatures with jointed limbs and an outer skeleton. They lived over 510 million years ago.

Trilobite fossil

OWN GOAL?

Crabs sometimes use their small, jointed legs to kick food into their mouths! They use their main pincers to break food down into bite-size pieces.

HEAVYWEIGHTS AND HORSES

Now you know about fish and shell creatures, but there are some other amazing sea creatures that you shouldn't miss out on.

BIGGEST AND FIERCEST!

• Lobsters have been known to live for 50 years and can weigh 20 kg (44 lb).

• The largest crab is the Japanese spider crab whose legs can reach an awesome 4 m (13 ft).

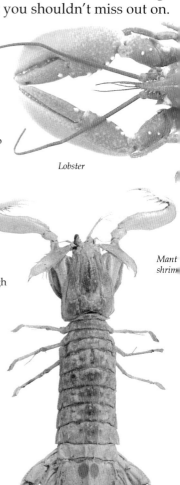

Lobster

• The mantis shrimp can bash its way out of a fish tank with one hefty blow! Yikes!

Mantis shrimp

TURTLES

Turtles can glide through the water. They come ashore to lay their eggs in the sand, but sadly, only one in a hundred of the babies will survive.

DEEP DIVER

The deepest diving turtle can go down to 1,200 m (3,937 ft).

SEA HORSES

Sea horses won't win many races! These elegant creatures get their name because of their horse-like shape, but there the similarity ends.

Sea horses live in seaweed or corals, as they don't like being out in the open water. They swim upright, moving along as waves pass down the *dorsal fin* (on their back).

Sea horse

Curiously, it is the sea horse father who carries the eggs inside a special pouch, until they are fully developed.

URCHINS

Sea urchins are covered in spines which they use to move around. They can be beautiful colours and strange shapes, but they are very painful if you stand on one!

Sea urchin

TEEMING MASSES

The oceans are teeming with teeny-tiny critters that you can't even see. The most prolific plants in the oceans, if seen under a microscope, look more like tiny fish! These little plants have a very large name – *phytoplankton*, usually shortened to plankton.

FOOD CHAIN PHENOMENON

Phytoplankton have an importance way beyond their size, as they are at the bottom of the *food chain*. Here's how it works:

Phytoplankton are eaten by *zooplankton* (swarms of tiny animals) – which are eaten by small fish (like herring) – which are eaten by bigger fish (like dogfish) – which are eaten by even bigger fish or dolphins.

Zooplankton

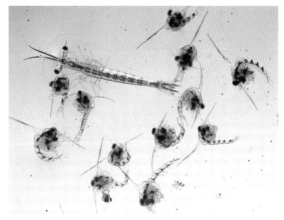

Some huge ocean animals, such as whale sharks and blue whales, cut all that out and just eat the zooplankton!

ALL DRESSED UP

There are many beautiful fish, but looking good isn't their intention. They are dressed to kill, or to avoid being killed. Their bright colours either camouflage them or warn off intruders or predators.

Mandarin fish

The mandarin fish looks like an upside-down bird with its low-slung fins.

The royal gramma fish lives in underwater caves. Its bright colouring probably helps to scare its competitors as it chases them away.

Royal gramma

SERIOUSLY WEIRD

Now that you have been introduced to some members of the sea creature family, meet some of their weirder relatives.

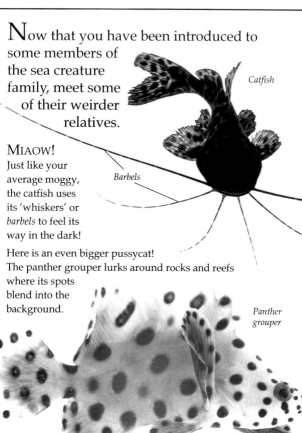

Catfish

Barbels

Panther grouper

MIAOW!
Just like your average moggy, the catfish uses its 'whiskers' or *barbels* to feel its way in the dark!

Here is an even bigger pussycat! The panther grouper lurks around rocks and reefs where its spots blend into the background.

CROAKERS
Drumfish, or *croakers* as they are sometimes called, can communicate over long distances. They make drumming and knocking sounds which carry far underwater. Once they get closer, they can recognize each other's striped pattern.

BLOW-UP FISH

The porcupine fish looks rather like an underwater hedgehog. One moment it looks quite ordinary...the next, WOW! It blows up to three times its normal size!

This porcupine fish would make a prickly mouthful.

SPLAT!

Rather like a water cannon, the archer fish squirts water at its prey, knocking it over to provide instant supper!

WATERY GLIDERS

Flying fish? Yes, really. They leap out of the water and skim along the surface by spreading out their side fins like wings.

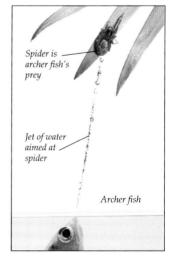

Spider is archer fish's prey

Jet of water aimed at spider

Archer fish

SCARY AND DEADLY

Here are some dodgy customers that you would do well to avoid. Some just look scary, but others are downright deadly.

DEAD NASTY

The lionfish, scorpionfish or dragonfish (to use three of its names), is lovely to look at but deadly to touch. It has spines on its back and under its tail, all tipped with a deadly venom. Ouch!

Lionfish

A STING IN THE TAIL

The stingray looks gorgeous with its huge 'wings', but beware! It hides in the sand, then cruises out to lash at its prey (or any passing human) with its thin tail, and then injects venom with its sting.

The electric ray can deliver shocks of over 200 volts to finish off its victims!

JET-PROPELLED

The squid uses jet propulsion to power through the water in the same way that a jet plane uses air to fly. Its body is streamlined to reduce drag, and if attacked it can zoom off!

Squid

SUPER SQUID

The giant Atlantic squid is the largest of all *invertebrate* animals (those without backbones). It can grow to more than 15 m (50 ft) in total, and weigh in at 2 tonnes. Gross!

To go with its huge size, the giant squid has HUGE eyes. Each one is more than 40 cm (15.7 in) in diameter.

FLOATING GNASHERS?

The scallop has eyes around the edge of its shell to detect passing fish. When swimming, it looks like a set of false teeth grinning!

Swimming scallop

LEGS AND EGGS

Here are some more fishy facts for you to digest.

AN ARM AND A LEG

The octopus sneaks up behind its prey, then pounces and wraps seven of its tentacles tightly round its victim, while keeping the one remaining tentacle anchored to the surface of a rock.

Another cunning octopus trick is to change colour within a second to hide from enemies. It can also squirt ink into the water while it makes good its escape.

MONSTER AHOY!

The kraken was a legendary sea monster with huge eyes and many tentacles, reputed to come up from the deep. Help!

TRAFFIC LIGHT TENTACLES

The beadlet anemone can be red, amber or green. Fully grown, it can have about 200 tentacles! 1, 2, 3, 4...

A GIANT FLOWER?

The largest anemones grow in tropical waters and can be more than 1 m (3 ft) across. Pretty big, huh?

Giant green anemone

EGG CASES

The female dogfish (which doesn't bark!) lays its eggs in an egg case called a *mermaid's purse*. You may find a dried-up, empty one washed up on the beach.

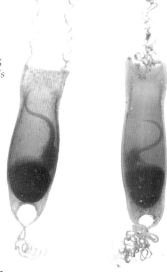

Egg cases with dogfish growing inside

BELIEVE IT OR NOT...

Genuine black *caviar* is fish eggs which come from the beluga sturgeon. It costs hundreds of pounds just for a teaspoonful and tastes very salty. DON'T ask for it for breakfast!

STANDING AROUND

The tripod fish is a bottom-of-the-sea dweller. It props itself up on two stilt-like fins and just stands around waiting for action!

Ocean Olympics

Dolphins love each other's company. They jump and splash about in large groups called *schools*. They are great show-offs and do all kinds of somersaults, backflips and acrobatics.

Fangs a Lot!
The shape of their beaks makes dolphins look as if they have a permanent grin on their faces! Those with long beaks can have as many as 260 teeth.

High Powered
Some dolphins can move at very fast swimming speeds. They do this by leaping out of the water whenever they need to breathe, rather than swimming along at the surface. This is known as *porpoising*...but porpoises don't do it! Confusing, isn't it?

River Cruise
Some dolphins never venture into the ocean. They are called river dolphins and they are much smaller than their sea-going cousins. They don't show off as much either, and usually only poke a beak above water!

CLICKETY-CLICK

Dolphins communicate with each other when swimming with a series of whistles and clicks. The sounds come from the nose, below the blow hole.

Bottlenose dolphin

ON PORPOISE

Porpoises are small relations of dolphins. Not much is really known about them as they are very shy, solitary creatures. Sadly, they are in decline as many drown when caught in fishing nets.

Porpoise

OPEN WIDE

The easiest way to tell a dolphin from a porpoise is to take them to the dentist together. Dolphins have cone-shaped teeth while porpoises' are spade-shaped.

SHARK AT BAY

The mere mention of a shark has swimmers heading for the beach. Aaagh! Here are fearsome facts for you to get your teeth into.

WHAT BIG TEETH YOU'VE GOT!
A shark never runs out of teeth! When its gnashers break or fall out, they are replaced by new ones from the row behind. During its life, thousands of its teeth will be replaced.

FOSSIL FANG
The massive fang shown here is the fossil tooth of a megalodon, an ancestor of the shark which probably lived 15 million years ago.

This megalodon fossil tooth is shown at only half its actual size.

BAD REPUTATION
In spite of their awesome reputation, only a few sharks are a danger to humans. There are only about 100 shark attacks a year and about 25 of these are fatal.

GENTLE GIANTS
At over 12 m (40 ft) long, the whale shark is the largest fish in the world. It is so gentle that it will let divers hitch a lift by hanging on to its fins. It feeds on plankton and its teeth are no bigger than a match head. Aah...sweet!

Whale shark is so big that it provides living space for large numbers of remoras (shark sucker fish)

CRUISING ALONG

Sharks swim gracefully through the water by swishing their tails from side to side, but they can't hover or swim backwards. They normally glide along at about 3 kph (1.8 mph), but when on the attack they rev up to about 25 kph (15 mph).

UNFAIR ADVANTAGE

Sharks have the same five senses as humans – sight, hearing, smell, touch and taste – but they also have a sixth sense which lets them pick up signals given out by their prey. Very handy!

GREAT, WHITE AND FAMOUS

The most famous and most awesome shark is the great white. Over 6 m (20 ft) long, it can eat a seal whole. Gulp!

Great white shark

A WHALE OF A TIME

Whales are not fish, but mammals, because they give birth to live babies which they feed with their own milk. Prepare to be wowed by some wonderful whale info...

GIANT SIEVE

Whales eat by filtering small fish called *krill* through giant fringed 'brushes' called *baleen*, hanging inside their mouths.

Years ago, ladies used to wear very tight corsets stiffened with baleen. Ouch!

GINORMOUS!

The blue whale is the biggest animal that has ever lived. The largest living animal on land, a bull elephant, could stand on the blue whale's tongue!

BELIEVE IT OR NOT...

A baby whale is already the size of an elephant when it is born, and at six months it measures 16 m (53 ft) long! It cannot filter food from the water at first, and relies on the milk from its mum. It guzzles about 100 litres (175 pints) every day!

Mother whale and her baby

BEACHED

A whale's weight is supported by the water. If it gets stranded on the beach, its internal organs are crushed by the weight of its own body, and it dies.

SPLASHING AROUND

Whales may communicate by leaping out of the water and coming down with a huge splash that can be heard many kilometres away. This is called *breaching*.

LOVE SONGS

A lovesick male humpback whale will sing a haunting song for hours to attract a female.

SLAPSTICK

Humpback whales slap their flippers on the surface of the water to make a loud splash. This is called *flippering*.

Humpback whale

TAILPRINTS

Each humpback whale has a distinctive pattern on its tail. A bit like a human fingerprint, no two are the same.

OCEAN PRODUCTS

Many things are harvested from the sea besides fish. Here are some of them.

PIPED ASHORE

Oil and gas are hidden deep below the ocean's surface in rocks on the sea-bed. Oil and gas platforms, with their *flare stacks* burning brightly, are a constant reminder of the danger when working with highly flammable ingredients. The oil and gas are sent ashore in special pipelines from the rigs.

NEIGHBOURS

An oil platform is like a small village. There can be as many as 400 people on board, living and working together. Some are *riggers*, who operate the drill. There are *geologists* (people who study the earth's structure) and scientists on board too. Probably most important of all are the cooks and cleaners who have to look after everyone!

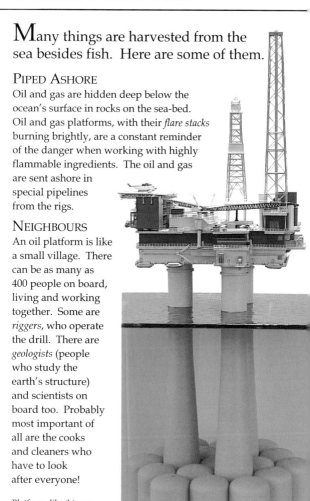

Platforms like this are built in sections on shore.

BATH TIME

Did you know that when
you use a natural sponge
you are washing yourself
with a soft skeleton?
Harvested sponges are
covered in soft, slimy
stuff – living tissue! The
sponge you use in the
bath is the bit left behind.

BLOWING IN THE WIND

The slate pencil sea urchin is protected by short, blunt
spines that were once used to write on slate boards in
school. Now they are collected to make wind chimes.

SEA SALT

When sea water evaporates, it leaves behind a crystal
crust which you then put on your chips – salt! Salt is
commercially produced in big, shallow pans.

WHALE PRODUCTS

The poor old whale produces this lot!

Whale meat extract used in margarine

Ground-up whale meat used in pet food

Whale liver used for its vitamin A

Sperm oil once used as a lubricant in cars

Oceans in Peril

The world's oceans are full of many wonders, but they hold dangers too – man-made ones. Here are some of the things which humans are guilty of doing.

Rubbish Dump

When a ship spills oil on the sea, the immediate disaster is obvious as dead and dying fish and sea birds are washed ashore, but underwater the damage can be even worse. The tiny, settling grains of sand and rock become toxic and can't support any form of life.

Poison Dump

Many poisons and pesticides are illegally dumped at sea. People can choose not to swim in polluted sea, but whales and dolphins can't read notices!

Rubbishy Beaches

A tremendous amount of rubbish finds its way on to beaches. Some of it will eventually disintegrate or be covered over, but some plastics are virtually indestructible.

WORST OF FRIENDS?

Dolphins and tuna swim together. When the fishing nets are put down to catch the tuna, the poor dolphins become tangled up too, and they drown.

EXOTIC ORNAMENTS

Souvenir hunters collect exotic shells because they are so beautiful, and can be made into ornaments and jewellery. People often don't know that their gift or souvenir has been taken from a living animal.

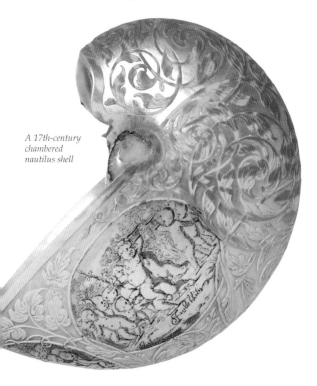

A 17th-century chambered nautilus shell

INDEX

Acknowledgements: British Museum; Exeter Maritime Museum; Museum of London; National Maritime Museum, Greenwich, London; Science Museum, London.

Picture Credits: (KEY: b=bottom, c=centre, l=left, r=right, t=top) Ardea London Ltd/F. Gohier: 43b; Bruce Coleman Ltd/Bob & Clara Calhoun: 36br; Jacana/F. Gohier: 43t; The National Maritime Museum, Greenwich, London: 12; Natural History Museum, London: 39b; 42b; Oxford Scientific Films/Max Gibbs: front cover tl; Planet Earth Pictures/Doc White: 38;/Keith Scholey: 46;/Marty Snyderman: 40b; Popperfoto/T Heyerdahl: 6; Tony Stone Images: 3t; Trustees of the British Museum: 8.

Additional Photography: Tina Chambers, Andreas von Einsiedel, Steve Gorton, Frank Greenaway, Charles Howson, Colin Keates, Dave King, Ray Moller, James Stevenson, Harry Taylor, Kim Taylor.

Every effort has been made to trace the copyright holders. Henderson Publishing Ltd apologises for any unintentional omissions and would be pleased, in such cases, to add an acknowledgement in further editions.